How to Do Great Works

■ ■ ■

Make it Happen

By Prince Handley

University of Excellence Press

Copyright © 2014 Prince Handley
All Rights Reserved.

UNIVERSITY OF EXCELLENCE PRESS
Los Angeles ■ London ■ Tel Aviv

ISBN 13: 978-0692252673
ISBN 10: 0692252673

Printed in the U.S.A.

First Edition

The only book you need on Exploits

2

TABLE OF CONTENTS

FOREWORD

This book will do the job **for you**. It will be your "walk through" companion: your consultant and mentor to help you accomplish that great idea you have.

For **great works**, you require: advice, discernment, warning, creativity, approval, provision, great wisdom, protection, health, direction, encouraging – and, above all – an anointing. You will find **all** of these and **how to draw from them** in this book.

This is a practical treatise: a "How to Do It" in simple layman's terms with **examples of what to DO and what NOT to do.**

But, not only for the layman, or inexperienced, this book is **also written for the person who has been successful**, but who wants to "go beyond" and "stretch out" in new uncharted ventures.

A danger of being successful is that one may overlook certain factors which could propel them to greater accomplishments. **This book approaches the aspect of doing exploits from the "outside in."** Most other books on this subject deal from the "inside out."

By using the external perspective, the author appropriates ALL of the possible aids in *How to Do Great Works*. The reader is NOT left wanting for help.

Get ready to **shake the world with that dream** of yours! The world is waiting on YOU to make it a better place. **You will be rewarded for doing so!**

How to Do Great Works

■ ■ ■

Make it Happen

REMOVE THE BARRIERS

Your personal sphere of influence -- through business, service, employment, ministry or philanthropy -- is at **the threshold of increase in quantum leaps** dependent upon what you do with the examples herein.

Much of the professional instruction in this book is designed for those who may be somewhat familiar with Biblical principles. However, there are **specific actions and advice rendered in this material which will help the reader accomplish exploits** – great works – regardless of the sector of lifestyle.

My assignment is to put you over -- to make it happen – in your life. I know in the future, when looking back, you will be thankful for the wisdom embodied here.

The Word of the LORD to you is:

> *Remove the constrictions. Expand your circles of influence. Break the old barriers. Expand your touch. Use your faith. I will bring it to pass.*

People need the breath of God ... the touch of God. You are the instrument of God to help people. Even your prayers for every nation, tribe, tongue, and dialect of the earth to be emblazoned with the glory of God are tools of LOVE and POWER through which the Holy Spirit works to reach people in time and space: sometimes years later in time ... and continents away in space.

I have known God to use video and audio casts, literature, and media broadcasts that were produced years before as instruments through which people were saved, healed, baptized in the Holy Spirit, and received MIRACLES **years later**. God honors His Word. He watches over it to perform it. *"Then said the LORD unto me, Thou hast well seen: for I will hasten my word to perform it."* [Jeremiah 1:12]

As I promised you, your personal sphere of influence -- through business, service, employment, ministry or philanthropy -- is at **the threshold of increase in quantum leaps** dependent upon what you do with this message. So be it, according to YOUR faith.

"Enlarge the place of your tent. And let them stretch out the curtains of your dwellings; do not spare; lengthen your cords, and strengthen your stakes. For you shall expand to the right and to the left ... " [Isaiah 54:2]

First, change your thinking. Think BIG. But *"new wine must be put into new bottles; and both are preserved."* [Luke 5:38] **Think PAST the limits of your mind.** Stretch out your horizon of ENDEAVORS and THOUGHTS. These things began Jesus both to **DO** and to **TEACH**. Base your thoughts, your goals, and your endeavors upon God's Holy Word. Use your faith!

■ Spend time MEDITATING God's Word so you can LEARN His principles.

■ Spend time PRAYING so you can talk to Him and HEAR from Him.

■ Spend time PLANNING so you will know what to IMPLEMENT for Him.

■ Spend time BELIEVING so you will know what to RECEIVE from Him.

Faith is wonderful ... but it's even better **when you have a PLAN to go along with your faith!**

If YOUR PLANS fit into GOD'S PLANS ...

you will have God's faith ...

and God's faith ALWAYS WORKS!

7

One time I took four of my oldest children on a hike. We had looked out our window for many months across a valley and to the beautiful hills where we lived. I kept telling them that sometime we would hike up to the hills. One Saturday I surprised them and said, Today is the day we will hike up into the hills. We packed a little lunch and set out upon our way. They were excited and I was, too.

As we reached the base of the hills we came across something we had never seen from our window. It was a deep stream, **which was an obstacle to our forward progress**. I carried my children one by one over the stream. **As we reached the top of the hills we saw a view of splendor**. It was a beautiful lake nestled in the top of the hills that we had never seen and did not know was there.

You will never experience the NEW (UNSEEN) vistas in life until you're willing to venture out.

Leave the "comfort zone" behind ... go into the Promised Land! If you reach obstacles ... which you will ... your Father will take you through **He will carry you across**. He will honor your FAITH. Just trust Him.

YOUR NEXT IMPORTANT MOVE

Do not be afraid of doing the wrong **right** thing!

Listen to God and make a decision!

This message is being written to you whether you are 5 years of age or 105. **When I was a little boy, about 11 years of age, I prophesied that men would travel to the moon.** No one ever dreamed, or talked about, such a thing happening. I also prophesied that I would be a minister when I grew up. The latter was probably more of a long shot statistically than the former (at least to those who knew me).

➡ Many years later both prophecies came to pass. Think **BIG** and prophesy **BIG** when you **know** it is God.

What stirs you? What makes you come to life? In a future chapter, *The Secret*, we will talk about spending time with God. When you do, things will begin to click in your life. **God will provide for you and you will be productive. He will provide NEW ideas!**

Change your thinking!

Do not limit yourself by your own thoughts!

- THINK BIG

- BELIEVE

- RECEIVE

- ACT

- MULTIPLY

- COMMISSION

9

Remember the acronym: True Blood Ran At Mount Calvary.

God is NOT old; He is eternally young. He is NOT limited, even by your disobedience.

In 2 Kings Chapter 7 we see the **productivity and success of anointed common sense.** There was a famine in the land. Also, the Syrian army laid siege to the Israelites in this area. Four (4) lepers were outside the city gates. They were facing death because of famine, just like the other people. But they were also vexed with an incurable disease: leprosy. The king and other people would not allow them to come into the city.

On a certain day the four lepers said to one another, Why are we sitting here until we die? **If we say, "We will enter the city," the famine is in the city, and we shall die there. And if we sit here, we die also.** Now therefore, come, let us surrender to the army of the Syrians. If they keep us alive, we shall live; and if they kill us, we shall only die.

When they came to the outskirts of the Syrian camp, no one was there. **For the LORD had caused the army of the Syrians to hear the noise of chariots and the noise of horses – the noise of a great army –** so they (the Syrians) said to one another, "Look, the king of Israel has hired against us the kings of the Hittites and the kings of the Egyptians to attack us."

Therefore the Syrians arose at twilight and fled; they left everything in their camp intact: food, silver, gold, clothing, tents, horses, and donkeys. They even threw away their weapons as they fled.

In 24 hours the economy changed: literally overnight. It had been prophesied by Elisha the day before (2 Kings 7:1). God found four lepers who had **spiritual common sense**. And, as soon as the lepers made a **MOVE**, God caused the Syrians to hear the sound of a great army.

➡ There are things that will never happen in life unless someone uses **spiritual common sense** and makes a **move** in faith.

➡ There are things in **your life** that will never happen until **you** use **spiritual common sense** and make a **move** in faith.

➡ If you are dying spiritually where you are at – if you are not productive – then use **spiritual common sense** and **make the move** after you have heard from God.

You may be in a situation now very similar to that of the four lepers. You are perishing spiritually where you are. That is, your life is not as productive as God wants it to be. You want BIG things to happen in your life: to help people and to make the world a better place.

TAKE A STEP OF FAITH: MAKE THE MOVE
ABOUT WHICH GOD IS SPEAKING TO YOU

What do you have to lose? Read the Word of God and LISTEN. Talk to Him and LISTEN. Pray in tongues and LISTEN. **Then do what He tells you**.

Jesus said, The field is the world. (Matthew 13:38-43) Jesus also taught that if YOU want to get the treasure out of the field, you have to buy the WHOLE FIELD. (Matthew 13:44) If you want to reach China, then you have to purchase the whole field. If you want to reach Iran, then you have to purchase the whole field. Meditate on this!!

Nothing happened until the four lepers took **THE MOVE** in the right direction.

Nothing happened until the priests of Israel took **THE MOVE** and put their feet in the River Jordan.

When you take **THE MOVE** of obedient faith ... then ... the God of Israel will cause things to happen. He will make a way for you!

Do not be afraid of doing the wrong **right** thing!

Your great work is going to have a dynamic of success that will expand in influence around the world. If it is a business venture, a technological project, an invention, or a ministry outreach, the fact that it will be anointed by God – you are asking for God's direction and anointing – **will bring favor to you and from people**.

Now, **connect your great work with God** by doing the following. Tell God that you will let this great work be used to reach people with the Good News of Messiah Jesus. If it is a ministry project then it is assumed that should already happen. If it is a business venture or other type of rewards based project, then promise God that because of His help in your success that you will give at least ten percent of your profits **from the success of the great work** to some good ministry that is reaching people and nations for Messiah Jesus. This way, you will also share in the miracles and healings and helps that people will receive around the world. **You will be helping confirm God's covenant** to bring the Good News to the world. **You're a double winner!**

Here's what God says:

"You are to remember THE LORD your God, **because it is he who is giving you the power to get wealth,** *in order to confirm his covenant, which he swore to your ancestors, as is happening even today."* [Torah: Deuteronomy 8:18]

➡ Now **you are working hand-in-hand with God** to be blessed so you can be a blessing. You can't lose!

The destiny of nations and people groups is hanging in the balance. Lay your left hand on your head and lay your right hand upon your heart and repeat these three (3) words:

NATIONS ...

NATIONS ...

NATIONS.

ANOINTING FOR SUCCESS

There are many ways God has to bring you success. Many times He or His Holy Angels are working ahead of time - or right on time - in unseen ways to deliver you, to prosper you, and to bring you into a place of super productivity.

Remember, God is FOR YOU. If you ever doubt this, look at the cross. *"If when we were His enemies He loved us so much that He sent His only Son to die for us, how much more, now that we are His friends, does He want to make us whole in every area of our lives."* [Romans 5:10]

God has every detail of your life covered. If you walk in constant communion with Him - if the Holy Spirit is your best Friend - and if you are involved in kingdom work, then you can expect His VERY BEST for you.

At times, the enemy may try to attack you through fear. Fear is a spirit. Fear is the opposite of love. God is love. Perfect love casts out ALL fear. *"There is NO fear in love; but perfect love casts out fear: because fear has torment. He that fears is not made perfect in love."* [1 John 4:18]

Speak to the spirit (demon) of fear; take your authority over it, bind it in Jesus' name and cast it back to the pit of Hell.

Use the Word of God against the enemy: *"For God has not given me the spirit of fear; but of power, and of love, and of a sound mind."* [2 Timothy 1:7]

There are times when the devil would try to come against you with a protracted period of fear. This may, or may not, involve people as agents of the enemy. This is a GOOD SIGN. **This tells you that what you are doing ... or about to do ... is scaring him**. The enemy is afraid. Since he is a liar, and the father of liars, then you know he is "bluffing you". Don't be afraid to "call his hand" just like you would in a game of poker. The difference is that you're going to use your Heavenly Father's resources (the BEST hand).

In a situation of protracted period of fear, do the following:

■ Fast;

■ Wait on God and listen; then,

■ Do what God tells you.

You may not even have to do anything. The fast may take care of the situation itself. And, remember: If you walk in constant communion with Him ... if the Holy Spirit is your best Friend ... and if you are involved in Kingdom work, then you can expect His VERY BEST for you. There are many ways God works for you and many of these are "behind the scenes" operations: "covert" if you will.

GOD IS ALWAYS READY TO WORK FOR YOU

"I will instruct you and teach you in the way you shall go; I will guide you with my eye." [Psalm 32:8]

Realize that this promise is both "individual" and "corporate". God is not only working for YOU, but also for those PEOPLE under your tutelage and leadership. **He wants you to KNOW His deliverance, direction, and dynamics: for your sake, as well as the sake of those people under your watch care.**

To make sure we are the recipients of His instruction, teaching, and guidance we need to be open to His leading and to be Spirit controlled. The verse immediately following the one above tells us, *"Don't be like the horse, or as the mule, which have no understanding, and whose mouths must be held in with bit and bridle."* [Psalm 32:9] This is why we need to be in God's Word every day, talking with Him, listening, and sharing our faith with others: to have understanding of His ways and NOT going our own ways.

GOD WANTS TO WORK FOR YOU

IF YOU WILL GIVE HIM THE GLORY

In the Book of Judges, Chapter Six, we read that the children of Israel did evil in the sight of the Lord; and the Lord delivered them into the and of Midian seven years. Then they cried out to the Lord and, as a result,

God raised up a deliverer named Gideon. Gideon had a band of 32,000 people ready to go to war. But God told Gideon, *"The people that are with you are too many for me to give the Midianites into their hands, because [your people] Israel will boast in a vain way saying, 'Our hands won the battle [it wasn't God]'."* [Judges 7:2]

GOD KNOWS HOW TO WIN YOUR BATTLE

JUST LISTEN TO HIM

God told Gideon, *"Whoever is FEARFUL and AFRAID, let him return and depart early ... and 22,000 people returned; and there remained 10,000."* Next, the Lord told Gideon, *"The people are still too many."* God then had Gideon separate the remaining people into two groups, depending upon how they drank water: if they bowed down upon their knees, or if they put their hand to their mouth and lapped the water with their tongues as a dog laps. God then told Gideon he would save them by the 300 men that lapped, and the other 9,700 were sent home.

You see, God wants to receive the glory for what He does through you, my friend. **You do NOT need a lot of big programs, you do NOT need a lot of people, you do NOT need a lot of money.** You just need the Spirit of God anointing you and directing you as you obey what He instructs you to do.

GOD CAN GIVE YOU A SIGN THROUGH ENEMIES

That same night the Lord told Gideon to go down to the host of the enemy because he was going to deliver them into Gideon's hands. The Lord told Gideon, *"But if you are AFRAID to go down then take your servant with you and you shall hear what the enemy says."* One of the enemy soldiers had a dream and Gideon heard him tell another soldier about the dream. The soldier said the dream was about Gideon, a man of Israel, *"for into his hand God has delivered us [Midian and all the host]."*

That is exactly what happened! That night the Lord gave Gideon and his band of men a GIANT victory. Only 300 with Gideon and they defeated the Midianites and the Amalekites and all the children of the east who were in the valley like grasshoppers in multitude; and their camels were without number, as the sand by the sea side for multitude. [Judges 7:12]

Remember: one person plus God is a MAJORITY! **Be watchful for those situations where God can invade the enemy through you and where God will receive ALL the glory!** The Lord can use those situations to bring **deliverance, prosperity, and wholeness to multitudes of people ... including YOU**. And God will be glorified because everyone will know you could never do these things on your own: they are MIRACLES!

"But thanks be unto God, which gives us the victory through our Lord Jesus Christ." [1 Corinthians 15:57]

THE IDEA

If you would stand on the ocean shore at the edge of a continent and look out at the horizon, what do you see? What do you think?

- How can I get to the other side of the world?

- How small, infinitesimal and insignificant I am?

- How limited are my abilities?

- How great is God!

Probably the latter will have the most impression upon your mind!

There are certain limits to **your** abilities ... **but NOT to God's!**

In the previous chapters we have discussed:

- *Remove the Barriers*

- *Your Next Important Move*

- *Anointing for Success*

In each of these we have attempted to layout a successful plan whereby you can accomplish things:

- That your mind has never conceived.

- That people (even yourself) said are impossible.

- That the enemy (the devil) said, You cannot do this!

Remember, the scripture says, *The things that are impossible with men are possible with God.* (Luke 18:27)

I am aware by the Spirit of God that I am writing to someone - a person or people - who have **an IDEA God has given you**; however, **you either**:

■ Do not know HOW to accomplish it (you need wisdom from God); or,

■ You are not POSITIVE the idea came from God.

➡ **First, the enemy of your soul will always lie to your mind if have an IDEA, or are working on an idea, to help people ... including yourself.**

➡ **Second, do NOT share your vision with others unless they are people who are involved directly in creative works of God.** Read the examples below to encourage you.

EXAMPLE 1 - On one website search of like subject matter, out of over 63,000,000 (that's million) like subjects, we were #1. Also, there were several sites where we were #1 out of tens of thousands. I give ALL the credit to the Holy Spirit. **I turned down every bit of advice** I received from media people directly involved with that industry. Some were friends. Some were experts with top credentials and experience in the field.

ASK GOD FOR WISDOM

DO WHAT HE TELLS YOU

EXAMPLE 2 - On one project that has reached some of the wealthiest Jews in the world and hundreds of thousands of people for the Messiah of Israel, **I was told by a government agency that I could NOT do it**: that it violated laws, codes, and restrictions five (5) different ways. **By God's grace, I did it.**

ASK GOD FOR WISDOM

DO NOT TAKE "NO" FOR AN ANSWER

EXAMPLE 3 - On one project the Lord gave me to do which has **reached hundreds of thousands, if not millions, for Christ in many languages** around the world, I was seeking feedback. I wanted the opinion, or advice, from someone. It was a far out IDEA and so I thought of the most far out person I was acquainted with to see what they thought of the IDEA. The person

21

told me, It is too far out for me! **That was my sign the idea was from God.**

ASK GOD FOR WISDOM

DON'T LISTEN TO OTHER PEOPLE

EXAMPLE 4 - Before I went on one ministry trip, a good close brother in the Lord told me, "You are NOT supposed to go on that trip." However, **I decided to do what God told me** and I went on the trip. By God's grace I reached many for Messiah Yeshua (Jesus).

Jews were saved, and **God crossed my path with a person who had information they passed on to me** before they died which helped me reach many, many Jews in Israel and around the world!

ASK GOD FOR WISDOM & FINISH THE JOB

EXAMPLE 5 - One project the Lord let me be part of - I actually only **watched** Him put it together - took only

22

one day! **All came together in one day: the IDEA, the money, the machines, the methodology, and the people.** I really had nothing to do with it except ride round with a lady in a Jaguar and go from step-to-step as the Holy Spirit directed. **Tens of thousands of Jews, if not more, around the world (many in Israel), have been reached for Mashiach.**

One Jewish businessman from Tiberius, Israel, flew all the way to California to meet me. I had an unlisted phone number; I don't know how he found my number. **He told me, *"I will pay anything to meet you."*** I met him and spent two hours in the Tanakh (the Hebrew Scriptures). The Ruach HaKodesh (the Holy Spirit) opened his spiritual eyes; **the man prayed and asked Yeshua HaMashiach (Jesus the Messiah) to come into his life and be his Messiah.** I then took him to the airline counter where he immediately booked a flight back to Israel.

SUGGESTION: When developing new projects, try to design them so they are NOT time-dated. That is, use graphics or photos or descriptive phrases (or, avoid them) so as NOT to render the projects "old fashioned" if someone is interacting with them years – or, decades – later. This can apply even to real estate projects, or architectural, projects.

ASK GOD FOR WISDOM

MOVE EXPEDITIOUSLY!

If Christopher Columbus had looked at the horizon from the ocean shore and listened to many others he would never have sailed to the New World 600 years ago.

What is YOUR horizon?

What is that stirring in your heart God has been activating? What is that IDEA the Lord has given you that you feel is humanly impossible?

ASK GOD FOR WISDOM!

Do what the Holy Spirit tells you. You may have a sense of the limits of your abilities but remember, *"With man it is impossible, but **with God ALL things are possible**."* (Jeremiah 32:27, Matthew 19:26, Mark 9:23, Mark 10:27, Mark 14:36.)

THE SECRET

Do you know your goals for God every day when you get up in the morning? Or do you have to struggle mentally to interfuse them with your daily schedule. Maybe you are a housewife, or a businessman, or construction worker. Whatever your vocation in life, **your REAL JOB** (that is, your spiritual job description) **was defined before the foundation of the world.**

No, I am not talking about serving God by living holy or being a witness for Christ; these are definitely part of the lifestyle of a real follower of Jesus: one who has had an actual rebirth spiritually at a specific point in time and space. I am talking about **fulfilling the occupational part of your ministry**, or more correctly, God's ministry through you.

You will never know this until you have spent a life defining period either alone with God or (in the case of a busy mother) in a time of consecration with God. **Your spiritual occupation will define your life goals** (both major and minor) and **help you in your decision making** processes (both major and minor): both long-term and daily.

After you begin operating in your spiritual occupation, **the LORD will from time to time revise or add to your responsibilities as you develop and show proof to Him of successful stewardship**. (Matthew 25:14-30) **He may even instruct and lead you into a completely different spiritual occupation after a period of time.** This is why we need to have times of refreshing that the Holy Bible mentions.

You must take off the wraps when you are seeking direction from God and instructions for your life and spiritual occupation. **Do not be afraid to THINK BIG. Realize that God may have something in mind for you that you have never considered or thought of.** That is where obedience comes into play. Also, **do NOT share your instructions from God with other**

people to get feedback. If you KNOW it is God ... and if it lines up with the Word of God ... then DO IT.

Lots of people have been led off the path of the will of God for their life by weird people ... and even by two or three confirmations of a wrong thing by weird people. By weird people I am talking about people who have no real productivity in their lives but who are always prophesying falsely to other people.

This is why you need to start every day by reading and communicating with God in His Holy Word and then in prayer. God has thoughts ABOVE your thoughts. His thoughts are NOT your thoughts.

"For My thoughts are not your thoughts, nor are your ways my ways, says the LORD. For as the heavens are higher than the earth, so are my ways higher than your ways, and my thoughts than your thoughts." (Isaiah 55:8-9)

This is where, again, it is important to take off the wraps! Do not just think outside the box! **God is NOT limited to three dimensions, or even to time and space.** Just read His Word and LISTEN! Just talk to Him and LISTEN. Just pray in tongues and LISTEN! This is why Ephesians 3:20 tells us that God is able to do **exceedingly abundantly above all that we ask or think**, according to the power that works in us.

That POWER in us is the energizing of our inner man by the renewing of the Word of God and the anointing by the Spirit of God as we listen, receive by faith, and obey. Here is where many people miss the mark: **OBEY**. We may be students of the Word, some even professors of theology in graduate schools; however, we may miss the mark of obedience. And, **missing the mark is equated with sin. We can be obedient in lifestyle and witness; however, when God directs us to take a definitive life style changing move, are we obedient?** Changing cultural settings or leaving our comfort zones are examples of such.

Isaiah tells us that the Word of God will not return void. It will cause you to be PRODUCTIVE in your spiritual occupation and it will make the way for your PROVISION. **You will be productive and God will provide for you!**

> *"For as the rain comes down, and the snow from heaven, and do not return there. But they water the earth, and make it bring forth and bud, that it may give seed to the sower (for production) and bread to the eater (for provision), so shall My word be that goes forth from My mouth."* (Isaiah 55:10-11)

Spend time in the Word of God. It won't return VOID. **It will accomplish in your life and in the earth (the nations of the world) what God pleases**. God's Word will prosper in the purposes for which God sends it. Why not be a channel for His Holy Word. The Word of God shall not return to Him VOID, but it shall accomplish what He pleases, and it shall prosper in the thing for which He sends it. (Isaiah 55:10-11)

The Hebrew word for **VOID** used in this passage is the word *racham* which means **"empty, without fruit or productivity."** So, if you want to know your spiritual occupation, and thereby make it a lot easier for your day by day decision making, and if you want to know life at the fullest -- the abundant life Jesus promised -- you, and if you want to be productive and see the provision of God in your life, then spend time in God's Word.

Spend time in the Word of God: for your sake, and for the sake of God. **What would you think if your children were so busy working but they never spent time with you? Many people in ministry are doing the same thing.** Busy about God's work but spending very little time with God. When we do this we not only lose out on fellowship with the GREATEST PERSON in the universe but we lose out on our own productivity and provision.

Spend time in God's Word and things will begin to click in your life. You will be in the center of the will of God. **God will provide for you. You will be productive**. You will have the joy of working at your REAL JOB: the occupational calling God chose for you before the foundation of the world. Remember, the thoughts of God are higher than your thoughts. But you have to KNOW His Thoughts!

The secret is in His Word!

THE BLESSING

In the previous chapters we have discussed:

- Remove the Barriers

- Your Next Important Move

- The Anointing for Success

- The Idea

- The Secret

All of these have been written to enable you to accomplish the impossible. The objective has been to render null and void barriers the enemy would attempt to impose upon you, and to empower you to receive birthings ... powerful, new ideas of the Spirit ... and then to implement these ideas.

The enemy of all righteousness wants to impose barriers in your life and thereby restrict, as well as constrict, your productivity in the Spirit. These barriers can be mental, physical, demoniacal, and psychological. They can be real or imagined. The enemy may utilize people, demons, lies aimed at your mind, conditions, or relationships. **Sometimes these relationships may even involve other believers**

If you know Yeshua the Messiah and are baptized in His wonderful Ruach (Spirit), you do not have to succumb to these oppositions and attacks. In 50 years of service I have found that many of God's people are clandestinely held back from their maximum potential **by not only a lack of stretching out in faith but also by focusing on the negatives instead of the positives**. They are in defensive mode. Just as in sports, the BEST defense is a GOOD OFFENSE!

On the cross, Yeshua became a curse for us that we might receive the blessings of Abraham. Notice, the Messiah of Israel became a curse for us that we might be blessed. He took on Himself the curse that originated with Adam in the Garden of Eden. **He took on Himself every one of the curses that are encompassed by that disobedience** of our first father: the first man, the first Adam.

The root of ALL curses on Planet Earth originated with the sin of disobedience by Adam in the Garden of Eden when he disobeyed God and obeyed Satan. When Adam did this, he relinquished his rulership of Planet Earth and yielded it to the Evil One. Notice, **there is NOT a curse on earth that does NOT originate as a result of that ONE ACT of disobedience!**

In Torah, Genesis Chapter 3, we read of a prophecy concerning the Seed of the first woman, Eve. **Her seed would defeat, destroy, and subjugate the tempter, Satan**, who deceived Adam in the Garden of Eden. This prophecy was pertaining to the 2nd Adam, **the Son of God**, who **would come to delete the curse and install the blessing(s) which were already programmed before the foundation of the world: the BLESSINGS originating from GOD.**

You were redeemed with the precious atonement BLOOD of Messiah, as of a lamb without blemish and without spot, who truly was FOREORDAINED BEFORE THE FOUNDATION OF THE WORLD, but was manifest in these last times for you. **The BLESSING was PLANNED FOR YOU before God created the world**. The universe was created for Planet Earth, and Planet Earth was created for YOU!

The ROOT of ALL blessing(s) ON EARTH - and ultimately in Heaven - was purchased by Messiah FOR YOU on the cross stake through His shed BLOOD and thereby deleting the curse. **Through His resurrection He installed the blessing**.

It was the first man, Adam, who initiated the curse through DISOBEDIENCE to God. It took a man (the Son of God) to delete the curse through OBEDIENCE to God so that we (mankind) could be BLESSED.

In the window of time between the fall of man in the garden with the resultant CURSE -- and the death and resurrection of Messiah with the resultant LEGAL installation of the BLESSING -- God made a WAY for man to APPROPRIATE His blessing(s). **That WAY was the same process by which men, women, and children appropriate God's blessing(s) today: the WAY of FAITH.**

Enoch, Abraham, Sarah, Deborah, Joseph, Moses, Elijah, Elisha, Daniel ... and many others ... appropriated the blessing(s) through faith. Read

31

Hebrews Chapter 11 in the Brit Chadashah (the New Testmament, or New Covenant).

In Genesis 12:1-3 God told Abraham: *"And I will make of you a great nation, and I will bless you, and make your name great; and you shall be a blessing: and I will bless them that bless you, and curse him that curses you; and in you shall all the families of the earth be blessed."* Later, in Genesis 22:18, God told Abraham, *"In thy seed shall all nations of the earth be blessed. Because you have obeyed my voice."*

The SEED of Abraham (the Messiah Yeshua) became a curse FOR US that we might be blessed with faithful Abraham. **The SEED (Messiah Yeshua) broke ALL the curse(s) ... even the ROOT of the curse(s)** imposed in the garden of Eden with the resultant sin, death, effects of witchcraft, sins of the father, generational curse(s) ... **so that ALL people could be FREE from the curse(s) and be recipients of the blessing(s).**

"Messiah has redeemed us from the curse of the law, being made a curse for us: for It is written, Cursed is everyone that hangs on a tree, so that the BLESSING of Abraham might come on the non-Jews (Gentiles) through Yeshua HaMashiach." (Brit Chadashah: Galatians 3:13-14)

Romans 4:13 tells us *"**The promise** that he (Abraham) should be the heir of the world, **was NOT** to Abraham, or to his seed, **through the law, but through** the righteousness of **FAITH**."*

Just as God works through FAITH, the enemy of your soul works through FEAR. The MIRACLES of God ... salvation, healing, power, commissioning ... all work through FAITH. The evil of satan ... witchcraft, disease, spiritual impotence, confusion ... all work through fear.

The BLOOD of Messiah is your covering! The BLOOD will protect you from the works of the enemy. The BLOOD of Christ is living. The life of God is in THE BLOOD. The enemy can NOT come beyond the blood line. In Revelation 12:11 we read: *"They overcame him (the devil) by the BLOOD of the Lamb, and by the word of their testimony, and they loved not their lives unto the death."* **If the BLOOD is your covering, you are protected. Speak (declare) the BLOOD over yourself, your family, your property, and everything the Lord has placed in your hands and the domains over which you preside**.

In the Torah, Moses told Aaron: *"Take your censer, and put fire therein from off the altar, and lay incense thereon, and carry it quickly to the congregation, and make **atonement** for them: for there is wrath gone out from the LORD; the plague is begun."* (Numbers 16:46) The Hebrew word here used for **atonement** is **kaphar**, and means **to cover, to cancel, to make atonement, to disannul**.

In the Torah we read: *"For the life of the flesh is in the blood; and I have given it to you on the altar to make atonement for your souls: **for it is the blood that*** *makes atonement for the soul (by reason of the life)."* (Leviticus 17:11)

It is the BLOOD of MESSIAH -- the one time, supreme, FINAL sacrifice to God for the souls of men -- that atones for your soul. **It covers you and secures THE BLESSING.**

A good personal friend of mine, Rachmiel Frydland, who is with the Lord now, **would sneak into the Warsaw ghetto during World War II.** Rachmiel was Jewish and he would sneak into the camp and declare the Gospel and **then sneak back out.** He prayed with many of his Jewish brethren who received Yeshua as their Messiah before they were murdered: some were murdered the very next day after he was there! I had the privilege to be in his home several times and to have wonderful fellowship with him. **Rachmiel knew the importance of the BLOOD of Jesus.**

Do not worry about any generational curses or curses from the bloodline of your relatives and forefathers. BREAK THEM with the BLOOD of Messiah! **Do not fear about some witch or someone placing a curse on you ... fear is a tool of the enemy.** The Holy Bible says, The curse causeless shall NOT come. **If you have done something wrong then confess it to God, ask for forgiveness and cover yourself with the HOLY BLOOD of MESSIAH.**

You are God's property and the BLOOD of MESSIAH is your COVERING if you will declare it so in faith. **Enjoin the blood of the covenant. Instruct THE BLOOD to be applied to yourself and situations BY**

FAITH. Prohibit the enemy and his people or demons from performing an action against you or your loved ones by your SPOKEN injunction of FAITH. It is a legal injunction purchased by the Lord Jesus the Messiah (Yeshua HaMashiach) on the cross stake and imposed by your faith. ATTACH The Blood, JOIN The Blood, IMPOSE The Blood to yourself, your loved ones, and your situation.

Request of the Father in Heaven to cover you and your situation with the BLOOD of MESSIAH. In the name of Yeshua (Jesus) charge verbally the enemy AND his power to be broken off your life and in your situation.

It is a direct command with authority. You have the POWER in the name of Yeshua to exercise authoritative or dominating control or influence over the devil and his works of darkness. Yeshua purchased this power for you, and commissioned you with this apostolic power to go:

▣ Preach and teach the Good News;

▣ Heal the sick; and,

▣ Cast out demons.

➡ **KEY:** You can do this with the Great Work(s) you are planning. For example, if it is a real estate project or a new industry, use your profits to help God's servants to preach His Good News. You can reach the world for Messiah with your next invention.

Be FREE from doubt. Believe in the abilities and power the Lord Jesus has purchased for you by His death and resurrection!

You have been granted this power inherently by **THE BLESSING** from the administrative unit of the throne of Heaven. **This is POWER delegated from Heaven to you!** The blessings of Abraham are yours. You rule as a king in life through Yeshua HaMashiach.

THE COVERING

In the previous chapters we have discussed:

- Remove the Barriers

- Your Next Important Move

- Anointing for Success

- The Idea

- The Secret

- The Blessing

All of these have been written to enable you to **accomplish the impossible,** to render null and void the barriers the enemy would attempt to impose upon you, **and to empower you to receive birthings: powerful, new ideas of the Spirit; and then to implement these ideas.**

The enemy of all righteousness wants to impose barriers in your life and thereby restrict, as well as constrict, your productivity in the Spirit. These barriers can be mental, physical, demoniacal, and psychological. They can be real or imagined. The enemy may utilize people, demons, lies aimed at your mind, conditions, or relationships. Sometimes these relationships may even involve other believers.

If you know Jesus, The Messiah, and are baptized in His wonderful Spirit, you do not have to succumb to these oppositions and attacks. YOU CAN DO WHAT THE ENEMY TELLS YOU CANNOT BE DONE. **You can do what many people tell you cannot be done**. If God is giving you, or has given you, an idea to reach people and nations for Messiah, then expect opposition. However, **expect VICTORY over the opposition**.

You are the servant of the Most High God, and if you seek God for WISDOM, God will give it to you. He will also **give you power** to do what He has assigned you and **send Holy Angels to assist you**.

The God of Israel is a **God of power who loves you**. He will **provide** for you and make you **productive** in and by His Holy Spirit. Neither is your success in question nor is the direction of God in your life in question. These are **given factors** as you meditate in the Word of God, pray, listen, and obey. Study again *The Secret* and *Your Next Important Move* in previous chapters. The **KEY FACTOR** to consider now is **YOUR COVERING**.

Your covering is NOT a man or person. Your covering is NOT your synagogue, church or fellowship. **Your covering is THE BLOOD OF MESSIAH!** The BLOOD of Christ is alive. Speak the BLOOD over yourself and your loved ones every day. Speak the BLOOD over your children **clear to the end of your seedline** every day. Speak the BLOOD over the properties, possessions and wealth that God has placed in your hands – **and over your next GREAT WORK, even before it is started**. This is part of good stewardship.

Ministers are not making enough of the BLOOD! At times of attack upon your mind, or when the devil tries to make you doubt your calling in the Kingdom, speak the BLOOD over your mind.

Remember that the BLOOD of Jesus opened the grave. *"Now the God of peace that brought again from the dead our Lord Jesus, that great Shepherd of the sheep, through the blood of the everlasting covenant."* (Hebrews 13:20)

His BLOOD both fulfilled and satisfied God's Law and God's righteousness. Christ overcame the power of sin; He brought it to nothing. Death was defeated; its sting had been removed. The devil, who had the power of death, was defeated and the enemy lost all right over the Second Adam (Messiah Jesus) and us.

The BLOOD of Christ destroyed the power of death, the devil, and Hell. There is an organic -- a living -- union between the BLOOD of Christ and the Word of God.

They bear testimony of each other. **Where the BLOOD is honored, the Spirit moves**. The Spirit draws to Christ and then brings people to the BLOOD.

How do we take advantage of the power in the BLOOD? As in anything connected with the Kingdom of God: **through FAITH. Speak the BLOOD of Christ against the enemy. Cover yourself and your loved ones with the BLOOD daily**. You cannot expect too much from the BLOOD of Christ; however, you will avail yourself of only those benefits of the BLOOD of which you have knowledge. Study what the Scriptures say about the BLOOD.

When you have received directions - ideas - from the Spirit of God, then SPEAK, declare, the BLOOD of Christ over the ideas. Speak the BLOOD of Christ over the birthings (ideas) you receive, and over the plans and the implementation of these plans as you move in obedience.

Remember this: when God sees the BLOOD, He will not allow the death angel to destroy. (Exodus 12:13,23) Do not let the devil kill the birthings which God gives you. Do not let all the time you spent alone seeking God and the resultant reception of the vision and its implementation be aborted by the devil and his *death angels* of whatever means they may originate.

People and nations are hanging in the balance. Be a good steward all the way to the end. **Do not quit!**

And, do not fail to appropriate THE BLOOD COVERING for you, your family, your associates, and your vision assignments from the throne room of God.

"By His own BLOOD, Messiah entered once into the holy place, having obtained eternal redemption for us". (Hebrews 9:12) You have been purchased - paid for AND purchased for God from the hand of the enemy - with the HOLY BLOOD.

This blood contains the LIFE OF GOD; therefore, **appropriate THE BLOOD COVERING for everything God has placed in your domain, and for the projects that have been birthed by your intense fellowship with the Father!** Speak the BLOOD over your work, and against the enemy, **NOW and in in the future (in advance)**.

➡ The **IDEAS** God gives you are for the impact of His Spirit upon Planet Earth. As you are faithful and OBEY to implement these ideas, multitudes of people will be blessed, and **YOU will be TWICE blessed because**:

■ **You are the channel through whom the Holy Spirit will flow.**

■ **You will receive the reward of obedience.**

This is HOW TO WIN!

THE FALSE COVERING MOVEMENT (FALSE DISCIPLESHIP MOVEMENT)

BRIEF CHAPTER INTRODUCTION

As you develop your great work – from idea through implementation and all the way through completion and monitoring – **you will have an enemy**. And, that enemy of your great work will be the same enemy as the enemy of your soul: Satan! WHY? Because: **that great work which started from an IDEA is going to bring you satisfaction, enjoyment, prosperity and freedom**. The enemy hates that; he hates YOU and anything that will bring you blessing from God.

Whether that great work you're going to do is a real estate project, a new technological device, a problem solving invention, a book or musical production, a ministry idea to bring healing to people, or a social project to help the needy ... you need to know the information in this chapter. **I don't want you to be robbed out of anything that has your name on it, and neither does God.** So ... listen up!

Never let a person -- or a ministry or a synagogue or a church -- be your covering! Many people who had a powerful call of God on their lives have been deceived by the **false covering** (false discipleship) movement. Many business people anointed by God to help establish his Covenant have been led astray.

41

Their anointing, creativity and production was diluted, the fire of the Spirit was quenched, and many millions of people were not benefited by the great work they were inspired to develop. This teaching will expose the teachings and the calamity of the false discipleship (false covering) movement, and **will protect you so that you can fulfill your destiny with power.**

In the late 1960s and into the 1970s there arose a **damaging movement** to the Body of Christ called *The Covering* movement. Another name for this group was the *false discipleship* or *false shepherding* movement. Satan realized he could **NOT** stop the great outpouring of the Spirit, so he devised a means whereby he would use a sector of the church -- and some Christian leaders -- to slow it down and divert it by diffusing its power and the intended Kingdom result.

There were several popular teachers involved in this movement. Their teaching went to excess so far as to be used by Satan to **quench true evangelistic and prophetic ministry** -- and at the same time **impede new ideas and projects from their development** -- with the result that false prophetic ministries came into being.

Many business and lay people that should have become millionaires were left impoverished and discouraged. Many creative and powerful new ministries never got off the flight deck. Anointed ideas and anointed people were "aborted" by the false teachers in the "shepherding" movement.

Here's a few of some of the excesses I know of:

➡ I knew a pastor who was near death in the hospital. A person was taking the pastor flowers and was told they must first **submit the idea** to elders.

➡ I knew a young man who left the Midwest and came to the West Coast of the USA extremely discouraged. He had a flourishing and powerful youth ministry. He felt the Lord leading him to start a church, however, the pastor and elders of his church told him **not** to start it.

A well known pastor friend of mine called me and asked me if I would come counsel the young man. I had just returned from a very exhausting six weeks in Africa and told my friend I would pray about it. On the third day, I called my friend and said, "*The Lord wants me to counsel the young man.*" I went to the home of the pastor, and during dinner the Spirit came upon me. I spoke to the young man and give Him the directive from the Lord: "***Go back there and start a church!***"

That church has grown so large it has three (3) locations in two states (at the boundary of two states). That church has, I think, **over 10,000 people** now and has been sending missionaries all over the world.

➡ I knew a powerful pastor who also had a ministry gift of evangelism. This pastor had ministered for years and moved into a new geographic area. He felt God leading him to evangelize at the local university. During the time of his getting acquainted in the new city he was fellowshipping with some brethren in a local church. He thought it would be nice to invite them to evangelize with him.

The elders of the church were involved in the (false) *covering* movement and told him **NOT** to evangelize at the university. When he asked them what they would do IF he did so, they answered, *"We will come against you with everything we have in the name of Jesus!"* **This man was one of the greatest pastors I have ever known**, and who also **worked with some of the best missionary organizations** in the world.

Many young people, and older people coming into the call of ministry – as well as people launching new businesses and projects -- were **kept from fulfilling the will of God** in their lives, as well as **hindered from being used to maximum potential** by the Lord. And many of God's People with dynamic ideas for business were led astray by inordinate control from other people, false prophecies and stupid (inaccurate) advice, deemed to be "from God."

During the 1970s **the Lord sent me around the USA and to other countries to expose this false teaching**. Lots of precious ministries were saved from shipwreck. I can think of pastors who each **have thousands of people in their congregations now** who were under the bondage of the *false* covering **movement**, and who saw the light as God used me to expose it. These young men and women went on to

OBEY what the Lord was telling them and **started their own ministries with the result of cities and nations being reached for Christ.**

They came out of spiritual bondage -- the trap of Satan -- **into FREEDOM of service and creativity!**

The examples I gave you previously are just of few of the multitudinous extremes of this Satanic strategy.

The **reason** that Satan tries to get people deceived into the *false* covering (aka: "shepherding") trip is because he **was once** the *anointed cherub who covers* ... and NOW **he does NOT want anyone under the covering of Jesus Christ.** (Ezekiel 28:14-15)

Man is **NOT** your covering; neither is a ministry or a synagogue or a church. If you think so**, try this**: The next time you start to get into a wreck or have an accident, see whose name you call on: a church, a synagogue, a rabbi, a minister, or **JESUS!**

When the BLOOD in the Tabernacle was placed by the High Priest upon the mercy seat in the Holy Place it effected atonement. The Hebrew word for *atonement* is *caphar* and is a primitive root which means *to cover, (figuratively) to cancel, to cleanse, be merciful, to forgive, and to purge.*

Once a year the High Priest would go into the Holy of Holies with the BLOOD of the sin offering of the atonements. It was most holy unto the LORD. The Hebrew word here used for *atonements* is **kippur** and means *expiation* (in the plural), or *a satisfaction, or to appease for guilt or sin by sacrifice.* (Exodus Chapter 30) *Caphar* and *kippur* both derive their meaning from the same Hebrew root form.

It is the same word from which the High Holy holiday Yom Kippur (Day of Atonement) derives its meaning.

Make sure that the BLOOD of Jesus the Messiah is your covering.

Lucifer was once the *anointed cherub who covers* and had authority and responsibility to protect and defend the holy mountain of God. Ezekiel 28:13 alludes to the possibility that part of his duty was to lead the choirs of Heaven in the worship of God. However, the scripture shows **he wanted glory for himself** and was cast down. Many in the *false* covering movement want *glory for themselves.* They are taking the position of God **telling the people of God WHEN, HOW, and WHERE they can serve** - even to the extent of telling them **NOT** to serve or minister.

It is interesting to note that in The Revelation of Jesus the Messiah to John on the island of Patmos, the Lord commended the Church of Ephesus by saying:

"But this you have, that you hate the deeds of the Nicolaitans, which I (Jesus) also hate." (Revelation 2:6)

He also told the Church of Pergamos: *"You also have those who hold the doctrine of the Nicolaitans, which thing I hate."*

The word *Nicolaitans* is a combination of two Greek words: *nikos* (meaning conqueror or victory) and *laos* (meaning people), which combination means **people conquerors**, or *conquering the laity*.

Christ is saying here that he hates the *false* ministry of *people conquerors*. **What the Holy Spirit starts, He wants to complete.** Jesus purchased His people with His own BLOOD, and He does NOT want people -- especially those who call themselves ministers of the Gospel -- putting Christians in bondage and trying to own or control the people and the work the Holy Spirit wants to do through them.

Ministers of the Gospel are to encourage and direct those the Spirit is calling and sending.

Do **NOT** let men take the place of the Holy Spirit in your life, your ministry or in your vocational calling – or in the great work God has put in your heart to do!

Let Messiah Jesus and His shed BLOOD be your covering. Align yourself through faith with His WILL and His PROTECTION. God, the Creator, wants to create through YOU by giving you IDEAS, direction and provision. Don't let men hinder the great work! You can **achieve the maximum** by listening to and obeying what God directs you to do!

THE TRIANGLE OF SUCCESS

What would you like to attain for the Lord in your ministry, your life, your family, or your business that you have not been able to attain in the past?

- What is on your wish list?

- What would you change about your present situation?

- What are your pains and unfulfilled wants?

The Psalms minister to us to help and direct, as well as to evoke worship. Psalm 37:4 says, *"Delight yourself also in the Lord, and He will give you the desires of your heart."*

The Hebrew word for **"delight"** is **"anag"** and **it means to be "pliable" and also to "delight yourself."** In other words ENJOY the MESSIAH. Have fun with the Lord, and don't be so tight or bound up that you can't express pleasurable emotion toward Him. If you enjoy him and have pleasurable emotion toward Him, He will grant you the petitions of your inner most being, even your thoughts and intellect.

No matter how much you've been used by God in the past -- no matter how much Bible knowledge and training you have -- and no matter how much favor you have with people, **there are three (3) things that can make you MORE SUCCESSFUL ... or break you:**

- **Friends**;

- **Thoughts**; and,

- **Time**.

The Holy Bible tells us: *"And if one prevail against him, two shall withstand him; and a threefold cord is not quickly broken."* [Ecclesiates 4:12]

Learn to ENJOY the Lord and to engage yourself positively in the three (3) areas above.

➡ FRIENDS

Who are your close friends and associates? Do they contribute to your intellectual and spiritual well being?

There are four (4) types of relational space:

- Public;

- Social;

- Personal; and,

- Intimate.

Public space is usually the space that's 12 feet and beyond. But it can be as close as the cashier at the grocery store. In an elevator it might be closer.

Social space is usually four to 12 feet and would normally be experienced at settings like school or social activities. Eye contact and gestures help feed it.

Personal space is usually 18 inches to 4 feet and normally found in friendship type relationships.

Intimate space can be from touching to 18 inches and is usually experienced with someone who knows the challenging aspects of your life. There is also "naked" space which refers to "emotional" space. This is a relationship, or situation, where your level of vulnerability is very high.

Today, there is a lot of teaching, and many books being written, on the subject of mentoring. However, **remember that Jesus is the only perfect mentor**. He is a friend that sticks closer than a brother! It's easy to be hurt in the fast paced world we live in today; but even in tribal areas where I have ministered there is hurt and hatred, sometimes decades and centuries old.

In the USA there has long been a series of stories, songs, and cartoons about the *Hatfields and McCoys*, feuding families in the hill country. Many people think it is a fictional story made up by writers; however, **it is true**. In 1878 Randolph Hatfield allegedly stole a pig (swine) from the McCoy family. Eleven (11) people were killed in the 10 years between 1882 and 1892.

Finally, after 125 years, the two families signed a document -- a covenant before Almighty God -- publicly forgiving and releasing each other.

Proverb 13:20 tells us, *"He that walks with wise men shall be wise: but a companion of fools shall be destroyed."* I am sure you know this already, but **examine your friendships**. Do NOT associate closely with those who have a problem with anger, laziness, talk too much, or are loose with their morals.

Also, **do NOT associate with those people who keep reminding you of past sins** you've already dealt with and for which you've asked forgiveness. They may even be relatives, or those who have been in close relational space as outlined above. **These people are doing what God won't even let Satan do: they are going beyond the BLOOD of Christ.**

The whole intent of the devil using them (even though they may not be cognizant of it) is to put you into a negative spin, to bring you down from the heavenly places (*Colossians* Chapter Three). **It is the devil's attempt to take you back into a place from which you have been forgiven, cleansed, and delivered!**

A reality check for the future: look at your friends. **Associate with other dreamers!** I would rather be alone with Jesus than to be with someone who didn't motivate and encourage me. **I want to be with people who sharpen my skills and intellect ... who "fan my flames" and enlarge my vision.** Three of the greatest inventors the USA has produced used to spend recreational time together in the woods and on picnics: Thomas Edison, Harvey Firestone, and Henry Ford.

Associate with the right people. If you don't have anyone with which to associate, then **email me your dreams and aspirations, or your problems**. I will be

51

glad to share with you. We are all working on the same team with the same goals. Send your email to: princehandley@gmail.com.

➡ THOUGHTS

Whether you realize it or not, **you are moving in the direction of your thoughts.**

Proverb 23:7 tells us *"For as he thinks in his heart so is he."* The Hebrew word here for **"thinks"** is **"shaar"** and is a primitive root **which means "to split or open" and to act as a "gatekeeper."** Don't open your mind to every thought that comes along? Satan is a liar and the father of lies [John 8:44] and **Satan has a mind oriented strategy to kill you, to steal from you, and to destroy you** [John 10:10]. The devil has two main weapons: deception and lies.

Your thoughts, like dreams, can **come from three (3) sources: God, yourself, or the enemy.**

If you believe lies from Satan or accusations from people, then you put barriers in your life. Do NOT dwell on them, but realize their source. Defamation of character and an evil report – especially after a person has repented and asked for forgiveness – is out of the pit of hell. It is one of the things that is an abomination to God. [Proverbs 6:16-19] Do not be a part of it. If someone is attacking you in such a manner, then pray and ask God what you should do about it. He may not

52

have you do anything about it, as the accuser will be severely dealt with by the Holy Spirit.

God still has GOOD things for you. **When one door closes, God always has a NEW ONE!**

"For I know the thoughts that I think toward you, says the Lord, thoughts of peace and not of evil, to give you a future and a hope." [Jeremiah 29:11]

Let God's thoughts fill your mind with life, hope, and positivity. Dwell on creative aspects of life and service.

"Casting down imaginations, and every high thing that exalts itself against the knowledge of God, and bringing into captivity every thought to the obedience of Christ." [2 Corinthians 10:5]

➡ **Refuse to retreat. Ask God to give you NEW IDEAS, new thoughts, and creative imagination to reach the world for Messiah.** Sometimes I tape large blank sheets of paper 27 by 34 inches (68.6 by 86.4 cm) on my walls just to write down new ideas to reach nations and people for Messiah Yeshua. I have found that either **just after, or during, a major attack from the enemy, the Lord usually blesses me with dynamic ideas** for reaching mass multitudes with the Good News of Messiah.

So when negative thoughts or attacks come my way, they are a "sign" that the enemy is scared, trying to discourage me and get me on a negative bent.

The enemy, being a spirit being, probably can recognize an anointing building up – ideas that will be formulated in my mind by the Holy Spirit – which will do great damage to the kingdom of darkness. Therefore, I rejoice for the glory of God that will soon be manifest to people in the tribes and families of the world! **How great is our God.**

I encourage you to do the same; **never back up ... stand still and listen to God's directions ... then advance ... and SEE the salvation of the Lord.**

When the children of Israel were trapped by the Red Sea with Pharaoh and 600 chosen chariots of war hot on their heels, Moses said to them:

"Do not be afraid. STAND STILL, and see the salvation of the Lord, which He will accomplish for you today. For the Egyptians whom you see today, you shall see again no more forever.

The Lord will fight for you, and you shall hold your peace.

And the Lord said to Moses, 'Why do you cry to me? Tell the children of Israel to GO FORWARD'." [Exodus 14:13-15]

Hundreds of years later, Jahaziel prophesied to the children of Israel with similar instructions from the Lord:

"You will not need to fight in this battle. Position

yourselves, STAND STILL and see the salvation of the Lord, who is with you, O Judah and Jerusalem! Do not fear or be dismayed: tomorrow GO OUT AGAINST THEM, for the Lord is with you." [2 Chron. 20:16-17]

➡ TIME

Previously I discussed the importance of time. We learned that **we need the Holy Spirit to anoint our time**. Our lives are made up of basic segways of days, in between which we sleep and obtain rest from the Lord. And, every seventh day is ordained from the Lord to bless us as a day of rest. [Isaiah 58]

During our waking hours **we need to spend quality time talking to the Holy Spirit**. The Bible depicts the Spirit as a dove. In Israel the dove was the turtle dove: a beautiful symbol of love, peace, gentleness, and innocence.

"And John bare record, saying, I saw the Spirit descending from heaven like a dove, and it abode upon Him (Jesus)." [John 1:32]

To understand the Holy Spirit more, we should **learn what a turtle dove is like**.

■ Turtle doves never fight. Pigeons do.

■ Turtle doves don't like noise. Pigeons do.

- Turtle doves like to be alone. Pigeons like crowds.

- Turtle doves are not territorial. Pigeons "bully" each other.

- Turtle doves can't be trained or domesticated. Pigeons can be.

- Turtle doves mate for life. Pigeons often have multiple partners.

Now if you want to be close to the Holy Spirit, to have wonderful communion with Him, observe His ways. Then, **prepare a nesting place in your heart for the Holy Spirit!** Spend quality time with Him. The more you honor Him, the more He will honor you! The Holy Spirit is God's agent on earth to supply the resurrection power of Messiah!

Learn to ENJOY the Lord so He can give you the desires of your heart. Engage yourself positively and wisely with:

- Your **friends**;

- Your **thoughts**; and,

- Your **time** of fellowship with the Holy Spirit.

This is the formula for **The Triangle of Success**. Use this with the other principles you have learned in this book. Now you know **How to Do Great Works!**

LIVE A LIFE OF EXCELLENCE!

Prince Handley

✦ ✦ ✦

NOTICE

Look for the companion book in the *Success Series* by Prince Handley titled, **Action Keys for Success**. Available at Amazon and other fine book stores.

Email prayer requests and praise reports to:
princehandley@gmail.com

Or write to:
Prince Handley
P.O. Box A
Downey, California 90241 USA

UNIVERSITY OF EXCELLENCE PRESS

NOTE

We listen to our readers. Tell us what **new** subject matter you would like to see published. Email your ideas to: universityofexcellence@gmail.com.